EARTH ALERT

W9-ATF-809

Edited by Nicole Carmichael

Written by James Marsh

WORLD BOOK / TWO-CAN

EARTH ALERT

First published in the United States in 1996
by World Book Inc.
525 W. Monroe
20th Floor
Chicago
IL USA 60661
in association with Two-Can Publishing Ltd.

Copyright © Two-Can Publishing Ltd 1996

**For information on other World Book products,
call 1-800-255-1750, x 2238.**

ISBN 0-7166-1739-0 (pbk.)
LC 96-06469

Printed in Hong Kong

1 2 3 4 5 6 7 8 9 10 99 98 97 96

Design by Simon Relph. Picture research by Debbie Dorman. Production by Lorraine Estelle. Thanks to Catherine Page and Marian McNamara

Front cover photographs: Panos Pictures. Insets: Planet Earth Pictures t, Bruce Coleman c, Survival International b.

Picture credits: Steve Bowles: p1, 13. Still Pictures: p3, 7, 8cl, 8/9bc, 9cl, 11tr, 14/15bc, 26l&br, 27tl&tr. Environmental Investigation Agency: p3tr 25tl. Zefa: p8/9tc, 21bl. Panos Pictures: p8cr, 9tr, 14/15 (main), 21tr. Greg Evans Picture Library: p9br. Science Photo Library: p10, 19. Survival International p15tr&cr. NASA: p20b. Planet Earth Pictures: p21c, 24br, 25cl. Bruce Coleman Ltd: p23, 24tl&r, cl&r, 25bl &cr. Natural History Photographic Agency: p25bc. Frank Lane Picture Agency: 25tr. Magnum Photos: p26tc. Environmental Picture Library: 27cl,bc&br, 31tc&cr. Arcaid: p31tl. Ford: p31br.

Illustrations: Steve Cross: p4/5, 24/25. John Davey: p6, 12, 18, 22, 30. Chris West: p16/17. Woody: p10. Brian Weston: p28/29.

CONTENTS

GLOBAL WA

THE EARTH'S IN DANGER
BUT YOU CAN HELP

Around half of Sweden's lakes are seriously damaged by acid rain. Waste gases from cars and power plants have also killed great chunks of forest in northern and eastern Europe.

By the year 2000 Mexico City will be the largest city in the world, with a population of over 25 million. Smog pollution is so bad there that a state of emergency was declared in 1990.

Because of chemical pollution in Canada's St. Lawrence Seaway, dead whales and dolphins have to be classified as toxic waste.

The world has changed enormously over the last few centuries. For many thousands of years life remained stable, the population stayed roughly the same, and animals lived without the threat of extinction.

But, with the progression of medical science, people are living longer and the world population is swelling. Every year over 92 million new babies are born, and each one needs food, clothing, and somewhere to live. As more and more of the earth's resources are used up, it's important that we all conserve for the future.

● Forests are being destroyed to make room for ever-growing cities, wiping out animals, plants, and entire tribal cultures.

● Harmful gases choke the atmosphere and eat into the ozone layer.

● Pollution plagues the planet's oceans and landscapes.

Half of the world's tropical rain forests have already been cut down. If the deforestation continues at the same rate, the rain forests will disappear in just 40 years.

RNING

Beautiful cities like Venice are under serious threat as sea levels rise because of the greenhouse effect.

In Russia, over-consumption of water from the Aral Sea has left ships high and dry. Fresh water is becoming increasingly rare.

Air pollution is so bad in Athens that cars are only allowed into the city on every other day.

Overgrazing has turned fertile land into semi-desert.

FOSSIL FUEL FORECAST

Once the earth's fossil fuels have been used up, they'll be gone forever. The trouble is, we're going through our reserves at an alarming rate.

Oil

Gas

Coal

2030 2060 2090 2120 2150 2180 2210 2240

● Oil is expected to run out by the year 2040.
● Gas is expected to run out by the year 2055.
● Coal is expected to run out by the year 2230.

It's high time for change. By reducing what we use and developing alternatives, we can conserve energy resources for future generations.

Despite all this, it's not too late to act, but it does mean that the whole world will have to work together. After all, it's a global problem. Check out the facts, then see how you can help make a difference. We've got a chance. Let's save the planet while we can.

ACTION!

Many of the world's problems are connected, but we can all do something to help. Throughout this book you'll discover ideas to help save endangered Earth

ZOO NEWS
Recently, zoos have come in for a lot of criticism, but they do a great deal of work trying to save endangered species. Today some species exist only in zoos. See if your favorite zoo has an adopt-an-animal program. In some zoos you can adopt anything from a canary to a camel!

START HERE!
The first step is to follow the three Rs — reduce, reuse, and recycle.
Reduce the amount of goods you use. Unnecessary packaging accounts for one-third of our garbage. Try to buy goods that have little or no packaging.
Reuse whatever you can. Keep scrap paper to write notes on; put a gummed label over addresses so you can reuse envelopes; and make dust cloths out of old clothes. Before you throw anything away, think if it can have another use.
Recycle what you can't reuse. Over half of our garbage can be recycled, including glass, metals, paper, plastics, and clothes. Many places have recycling programs. *More ideas on pages 12 and 18.*

BLEAK HOLE
As the hole in the ozone layer grows, widen your knowledge of the situation. On *page 22* you'll find loads of ideas on how you can make a difference today. Even something as simple as turning off a light is a step in the right direction.

CLEAN UP YOUR ACT
Don't throw away opportunities to wipe out pollution. You'll find the problem is littered around you, so get on the trail to *page 10.*

NEIGHBORHOOD WATCH
Most areas have conservation groups that try to protect and preserve the local environment. Your local library will help you find out which organizations exist near you and whom you should contact.

BRANCH OUT
You don't need a map of the Amazon to get to the root of the rain-forest problem. There are all sorts of national and international campaigns that you can get involved in. You can also take steps at home to help conserve the rain forest, such as spreading the message about mahogany.

More ideas on page 18.

THE PEOPLE PROBLEM

Over-population is the world's number one growing concern

Every second, three more babies are born in the world. That's 92 million new faces – or the same number as the population of Mexico – every year.

And because 92 million people aren't dying every year, the world is getting more and more crowded.

It took until 1804 for the world's population to reach one billion, but by 1994 it had rocketed to 5.6 billion. At the end of the century it's expected to have increased by a staggering 500 million people.

GROWING UP – AND UP!

The populations of some countries are growing at a much faster rate than others. In Egypt, for instance, there are nearly four babies born in relation to every person that dies. At this rate, Egypt will double its population in just 31 years.

It's vital that resources are maintained to protect these swelling nations.

BOOM!

The worldwide population explosion

In many Third World countries, people generally have very large families. One reason for this is that in the past many children died young.

Now, thanks to modern medicine, far fewer children die and, as a result, populations are growing. This situation is putting more of a strain on living resources.

In order to provide food and housing for all these extra people, cities are growing and more and more land is being used for farming. Every year, an area of rain forest roughly half the size of Pennsylvania is cut down to make space for more farms and villages.

Water supplies are also under threat. Some of the world's driest countries are in Africa and the Arab states – the regions where populations are increasing fastest.

The world community is now trying to educate everyone about the population problem. But it takes time for attitudes to change, and meanwhile the problem continues to grow.

AFRICA

Population: **700 million**
Time it will take to double: **24 years**
By the year 2025 Africa will have more than three times as many people as Europe. And in just five years, it will have to import nearly half of the cereal it needs to feed its growing population.

THAILAND

Population: **59.4 million**
***Time it will take
to double:***   **50 years**
Thailand is one of the world's population success stories. Thirty years ago Thai women were having six or more children each. But after an education policy was introduced in 1970, the birth rate gradually dropped to two children per family.

CITY LIMITS

By the year 2000 nearly half of the world's population will live in cities. This mass exodus from the country has already caused great areas of shantytowns to spring up on city outskirts. As you can see from this photograph of a shantytown in Rio de Janeiro, Brazil, it's a bleak life for the three million residents.

It's thought that by the time the world's population reaches 10 billion in 2050, we will need an extra 1.7 million square miles for farming and housing. That's an area half the size of the United States!

CHINA

Population: 1.2 billion
Time it will take to double: 61 years

New laws introduced in 1979 aimed to stop the baby boom. Now Chinese parents who have more than one baby lose out on government help and are also threatened with fines. Because of this, parents often keep babies secret, and it's thought that there may be as many as 100 million unreported Chinese people.

INDIA

Population: 911.6 million
Time it will take to double: 36 years

Despite government campaigns, India's population is still increasing. By the year 2000 it's expected to equal the population of China, with over one billion people. But with only a third as much land, it's in grave danger of not being able to grow enough food.

EUROPE

Population: 728 million
Time it will take to double: 1025 years

Europe's birth and death rates are evenly matched, so that the population remains constant. In some countries, such as Italy, Germany, and Hungary, the population is actually falling.

WASTE MATTE

The secret of recycling is a load of garbage!

▲ *Car-unch! Crushed car bodies can be recycled into shiny new machines.*

Every day, each of us in the United States produces about four pounds of garbage. Once it's thrown into the trash can, most of us don't give it a second thought – after all, it's only garbage, isn't it? Or is it?

You may not want it, but over half of what is carted off by the garbage truck can be recycled. Unfortunately, right now just a twentieth of household waste is being recycled – that means we could recycle around 10 times as much of our garbage as we do at the moment.

COVER UP

When garbage is taken away by the garbage truck, most of it is dumped in landfills, which are then covered over with soil – leaving the garbage to be broken down by nature. This takes a long time and can result in explosive gases being produced. In some places,

these explosive gases are collected to provide energy for heating, but not all of our garbage decomposes easily. Some plastics are expected to survive for at least another 400 years.

A much better alternative is to cut down on waste in the first place, then reuse the waste we do

RS

▲ *The garbage mountain grows, but there are alternatives.*

suited to recycling, but when it comes to energy savings, metals are the winners by a mile.

Humans have reused metal ever since they first discovered iron. Nowadays, over 40 percent of steel is made from recycled metal. In our household garbage, most of the unwanted metal comes in the form of cans. In fact, if the 16 billion cans that we use every year were placed end to end they would stretch to the moon and back – twice!

Cans are made from either aluminum or steel. Aluminum requires huge amounts of energy to produce it from scratch, but recycling uses 95 percent less energy – and that saves lots of money. That's why manufacturers are so eager to recycle your used aluminum cans.

Almost anything can be made out of recycled materials – from tissue paper, appliances, and outdoor furniture to a new BMW car, which is 84 per-cent recycled! However, it's

no use recycling garbage if no one uses the finished products.

So, next time you're shopping, keep a lookout for the various recycling logos on product labels. It certainly won't be a *waste* of your time!

produce. After all, recycling uses less energy so we can often save money. And the more we recycle, the less space we need to dispose of our garbage. Simple!

PRECIOUS METALS
The largest proportion of our garbage is paper and cardboard, which is ideally

COSMIC CLEANER

American scientists have started work on a special space-age vehicle to boldly clean where no cleaner has gone before. Litterbug rockets have jettisoned so much debris into Earth's orbit that it poses a real threat to future space missions.

ASPOD, or the Autonomous Space Processor for Orbital Debris, will grab a chunk of space junk, chop it up, and store it. Once full, ASPOD will reenter Earth's atmosphere at such a high speed that it will incinerate itself and the space garbage inside. Sounds a bit more complicated than cleaning up your bedroom!

CATCH THE LITTERBUG

Grab that garbage and start recycling today!

WHAT YOU CAN RECYCLE

PAPER:	*Newspapers, magazines, paper, and cardboard*
GLASS:	*Bottles and jars*
METAL:	*Steel and aluminum cans, aluminum foil, foil dishes*
PLASTICS:	*Drink bottles, detergent bottles, shopping bags, margarine tubs, yogurt containers, and food trays*
LEFTOVERS:	*Food can make compost, a great natural fertilizer*
CLOTHES:	*Old clothing and linens are welcomed by some social service organizations, such as the Salvation Army and Goodwill*
OTHERS:	*Batteries, car oil, and car tires can sometimes be disposed of through a local hazardous waste program*

CAN IT!

The best way to recycle cans is to separate them into steel and aluminum varieties. Most can labels say whether they are steel or aluminum – but if in doubt, get your magnet out. Steel is attracted to a magnet and aluminum isn't.

Once you've sorted out which is which, it's time to wash and squash – a quick wash to clean them out, then a careful squash with your foot or can crusher to make them easier to store. Once you've collected a good bag load, take them to your local recycling center. If you're a soda pop fan, your savings will soon mount up!

READ ALL ABOUT IT!

The first step to recycling paper is to make sure you use both sides. Try to think of uses for scrap paper, such as a phone message pad. Collect your old newspapers and magazines and take them to your local recycling center.

LOTTA BOTTLE

Take the lids off bottles, jars, and other containers and separate glass items into different colors (clear, green, brown). Most plastic bottles and other plastic items have a code stamped on them so that you can identify what type of plastic they are. Then it's off to the recycling center – but don't waste gasoline making a special trip in the car!

aluminum and other metals 9%

paper and cardboard 30%

glass 10%

fabrics 3%

plastic 4%

miscellaneous 21%

vegetable waste 23%

GARBAGE RATIOS

WOOD YOU BELIEVE IT?

Ten thousand years ago, half the world was covered in forest

Since then, over a third of those forests have been cut down to provide land for farms and houses – and most of that damage has happened in the last 50 years. Trees play a vital role on Earth, helping us breathe, preventing flooding, and providing shelter for literally millions of species of animals and plants. Isn't it time to stop cutting down forests and cut down deforestation instead?

DAYLIGHT ROBBERY

IT'S A FACT – an area of rain forest the size of a football field is destroyed every second. The bulk of this shocking deforestation is taking place in the tropical rain forests. Brazil cuts down over a third of the trees felled in the world every year – but it's not a problem that's confined to the tropics. Other precious forests all over the globe are also being devastated by logging.

BURNING ISSUE

When forests are cleared, a technique called "slash and burn" is used. Trees are hacked down and the rest of the forest is burned. This ruins the area and pollutes the atmosphere with smoke and harmful gases – more about that on page 19.

Trees and other plants take in the main greenhouse gas carbon dioxide and use it to grow, producing oxygen in the process. So when forests are slashed and burned, not only are more greenhouse gases created, but a valuable oxygen supply is destroyed.

Trees also soak up lots of water, which their leaves slowly give out as water vapor. In tropical rain forests, clouds actually form above trees because they produce so much water vapor.

Once trees are removed, flooding can become a real danger. In Thailand in 1988, loggers cut down thousands of trees, and torrential rain caused massive flooding. Fortunately, after the disaster commercial logging was banned.

TROPICAL TREASURES MAHOGANY

Money doesn't normally grow on trees, but it does for loggers – a single mahogany or teak tree can be worth $4,000! However, these trees don't grow in clumps – there may be just three in an area the size of two football fields.

Mahogany trees are also difficult to get at, and loggers often destroy the surrounding trees in order to get to the valuable ones with their machinery.

GRAZING LAND

Vast tracts of Amazonian rain forest have also been cleared to make way for cattle, to provide beef to eat. It's been estimated that for every hamburger sold, two rain forest trees have been destroyed.

A third of the land cleared for grazing cattle in the Amazonian rain forest has now been abandoned as useless.

Over the years it has been proved that cleared rain forest is totally unsuitable for grazing. The top-soil is very thin and held together only by tree and plant roots. Once the forest has been razed, the fertile topsoil is soon washed away. The clay layer beneath is baked by the hot sun and forms an infertile, concretelike surface that will never support the rain forest again.

MINERAL MINING

Miners are rain-forest vandals, too – they lay waste to the land in search of gold and tin. Not only do they destroy the forest, they also pollute the soil and rivers with their chemicals.

Unfortunately, it seems the very riches of the tropical rain forest have led to its destruction.

Replanting of trees does happen,
but at the moment just one square mile is planted for
every 10 square miles that are cut down.

THE PRICE OF LIFE

The Yanomani Amazonians have existed in harmony with the rain forest for centuries, but now they are in danger of disappearing forever.

The threat has come from outsiders who have started building a new road through the rain forest, plus prospectors searching for tin and gold. Because the Yanomani have no resistance to diseases, they have been infected with germs that the outsiders have unknowingly brought with them. As a result, many Yanomani have died.

Also, the rivers where they fish have been polluted by the miners' chemicals, and some Yanomani have even been shot because of land disagreements.

There are now only about 9,000 Yanomani people left. Unless the Brazilian government recognizes the land belongs to the Yanomani alone, the future for these tribal people is bleak.

But it's not too late to save the riches of the rain forest. Check out its treasures on the next page; then dip into tropical tips on page 18.

Staying green all year round, tropical rain forests are the world's most diverse environments

Over half of Earth's animals and plant species live in rain forests, and thousands of products that we take for granted originated there, including hundreds of different foods and many medicines.

1 The tallest trees can be as high as 200 ft. The smaller trees of 100–150 ft. form the forest canopy. This interlocking roof of branches is home to many birds, such as toucans and parrots, as well as monkeys and bats.

2 The sloth is one of the laziest creatures in the world – it can spend over 21 hours a day hanging around sleeping.

3 The harpy eagle, endangered by deforestation, lives in the tops of the highest trees and feeds on sloths and monkeys.

4 This beautiful golden lion tamarind used to be a common sight in the Brazilian rain forest, but due to deforestation it is now one of the world's most endangered species.

5 This bird-eating spider measures 7 in. (gulp!) between its legs and catches food by using its eight eyes to keep a lookout for small birds and insects.

6 Poison arrow frogs secrete a poison so deadly that just a tiny drop of it will kill a person. Amazonian indians use the tree frogs' poison on the end of their arrows for hunting.

7 The inch-long Candiru fish uses sharp spines on its back to pierce the flesh of animals or humans that come near it.

8 Some large herbivores, such as capybaras, tapirs, deer, and antelope, live on the forest floor.

9 Much of our fruit comes from the rain forest. We've all tried pineapples and bananas, but there are another 2,500 varieties that we haven't even tasted yet!

10 One in four of today's medicines originated in the rain forest. Scientists believe there are thousands more just waiting to be discovered.

11 Rubber comes from trees that originally grew in Brazil and are now cultivated in Asia.

12 Bromeliad plants grow on top of other plants. They suck moisture from the air and steal nourishment from their host plant.

▲ CANOPY

▲ MIDDLE

▲ FLOOR

IT'S A JU

NGLE OUT THERE!

TROPICAL TIPS

Rain forests are a treasure the world needs to keep. You might feel a million miles away from the problem, but you really can help

- Wherever possible, buy recycled paper products – you'll be helping to save trees.
- Recycle paper and reuse envelopes.
- Use cloth handkerchiefs instead of throwaway paper ones.

- Find out if your school has furniture made of hardwoods like teak and mahogany. If it has, organize a petition to present to your principal. It may make school authorities think twice about buying any more in the future.
- Reuse plastic shopping bags, and if you're buying small items, see if you can do without a bag and carry the item in your knapsack, school bag, etc.

- Organize a special fundraising event or do a sponsored activity to help one of the environmental organizations or your local conservation group.

- Look after trees in your local area by giving them buckets of water in dry weather.

- Avoid overpackaged goods.
- Help conserve local woodlands by joining conservation groups.
- Check that orchids at the garden center are home-grown.
- Put on a play about tribal peoples showing some of the problems they face.

- See if you can plant a tree at home in your yard, at your school, or on a vacant lot.
- If you or a friend need wood to make something, choose "good woods" like ash, cherry, and oak rather than endangered rain forest hardwoods like mahogany and teak.

- Make a poster about the rain forest and ask if you can display it at school.

WRITE ON!
One of the best ways to help tribal people and stop deforestation is to write a letter to the government of the country responsible. Write to the head of your government and explain why you are concerned about what's happening in the rain forests. Keep your letter brief and simple – and remember to be polite!

IT'S WARMING UP!

If it wasn't for the greenhouse effect, Earth would be a much colder place – a teeth-chattering 59°F cooler – but is it getting too hot to handle?

Earth's atmosphere protects us from the cosmic cold of space as if it were wrapping us up in a warm blanket. Like the glass in a greenhouse, the atmosphere lets the sun's rays through and then keeps the heat in – that's why it's called the greenhouse effect.

The gases that act as the greenhouse's panes of glass are known as greenhouse gases. They include water vapor (one form of which is cloud), carbon dioxide, and methane.

WARMING WARNING
For millions of years, these greenhouse gases have got on with their job without any problems, but in the last 100 years things have changed.
● Humans have been pumping extra carbon dioxide into the atmosphere by burning fossil fuels such as coal, gas, and oil.
● Vast areas of rain forest – which can absorb carbon dioxide – have been destroyed.
● Methane levels have gone up because of cattle and increased crop farming.
● Other harmful gases, such as CFCs and nitrous oxide, have been released into the already choking atmosphere.

The more greenhouse gases there are, the hotter the "greenhouse" becomes. In the last hundred years the world's temperature has increased by 1°F and it's expected to rise by up to 8°F in the next 50 years.

That may not sound like much, but scientists say this global warming will have a devastating effect on the planet's future climate.

The heat is on to stop global warming

THE HOLE TRUTH

About 10-20 mi above the surface of Earth, ozone gas forms a layer in the atmosphere. It usually blocks out almost all of the sun's ultraviolet rays, but in recent years this ozone layer has been getting thinner.

A group of gases called CFCs (chlorofluorocarbons) are being blamed. They're used in refrigerators and foam packaging. Until recently it was thought they didn't react with any other chemicals. However, when CFCs drift into the ozone layer, they are changed by the sun's ultraviolet rays and start attacking the ozone layer.

This has caused massive holes in the ozone layer above the Arctic and Antarctica. Now the hole above Antarctica is as big as North America and as deep as Mount Everest is high.

GLOBAL PROMISE

Most countries have agreed to stop using CFC gases by the year 2000, but as they last for around 100 years (and some for as long as 23,000 years), it will be at least a century before their effect is wiped out.

The thinning ozone layer is already being blamed for increasing cases of skin cancer and eye disease in Florida and California. It's also feared that the lack of ozone could lead to the failure of some crops. CFCs were originally called "wonder" gases, but they've just caused a "hole" load of problems.

It will be at least a century before the effect of aerosols is wiped out

Thermal image taken by satellite of the hole in the ozone layer

GREENHOUSE

FEELING HOT HOT HOT!

▼ *The threat of tornadoes is spiraling.*

CFCs don't just harm the ozone layer, they also speed up the greenhouse effect. They are up to 25,000 times stronger than carbon dioxide, and this makes them one of the important factors in global warming.

If temperatures rise because of global warming, the Arctic and Antarctic ice caps will begin to melt and sea levels will rise. The oceans have already risen by 6 in. this century and could rise by a whopping 3 ft. by the year 2030.

This would be disastrous for low-lying countries such as Holland, Bangladesh, and the Maldives, which would either disappear under water or find that their land is ruined because of saltwater flooding.

Sea life will also be threatened by a rise in the oceans' temperature. For instance, coral stops growing in water above 82°F and dies. This is called bleaching and has already affected corals in the Caribbean, Australia, and the Philippines.

STORMING IN

As global warming becomes more significant, the world's climate is expected to change. Northern Europe will find its weather becoming like that of present-day southern Europe. That might seem nice on a cold winter day, but the worldwide effect would be catastrophic. Parts of Africa, Asia, and America will suffer from drought, while storms will become stronger and more frequent the world over.

The forecast looks gloomy, but you can do something to help.

BRIGHT IDEAS

Do your bit to halt the greenhouse effect

● Unnecessary use of electricity causes more of the greenhouse gas carbon dioxide to be produced, so turn off videos, televisions, and other electrical appliances when they're not being used.

● Use public transportation where you can. Or even better, save money and energy by riding a bike or walking.

● Energy-efficient light-bulbs cost more to buy, but because they use less electricity and last longer, they are much cheaper in the long run.

● Get your parents to turn down the heating a notch and adjust it so that it comes on a little later. You won't notice the difference, but you will save energy.

● Try to get your parents to make one less journey in the car every week and see if they can share trips with anyone.

● If you know someone who is buying a new refrigerator, remind them to compare the energy efficiency of different models.

● Try to reuse and recycle as much as possible (lots of ideas on page 12).

CAR TROUBLE Every year, the average car produces four times its own weight of the greenhouse gas carbon dioxide.

● When you're shopping, look out for products with less packaging to cut down on waste.

FAIR FARES Even when a bus is only a quarter full, it's twice as efficient as a family car.

FRESH AIR? NO THANKS! Some plants, such as tomatoes, actually thrive on higher carbon dioxide levels.

GOING, GOING...

Gone! This Javan rhino will be history unless we act soon

At first sight, you might imagine this odd-looking animal belongs to the dinosaur age. Soon, it may have something else in common with dinosaurs other than looks. It may also be extinct.

It is believed that during the next 25 years half a million species of animals and plants living on the planet will become extinct. That's 20,000 every year.

Soon, books may be the only place to find animals like the Javan rhino, mountain gorilla, blue whale, and many, many more.

SUCCESS STORY

It is possible to save species. The numbers of Arabian oryx had dropped to just three wild animals because of hunting. Now, thanks to the World Wide Fund for Nature, there are over 800 protected Arabian oryx living in the wild.

WHOOPING CRANE

Population: 140. At one point numbers dropped below 50 as a result of humans hunting and building on breeding grounds. Careful zoo programs hope to boost numbers.

FLORIDA PANTHER

Population: around 3 Numbers are dwindling at an alarming rate as humans continue to take over their habitat in the Florida Everglades.

HYACINTH MACAW

Population: 3,000. Prized as a cage bird, the hyacinth macaw can fetch as much as $20,000 on the black market.

MOUNTAIN GORILLA

Population: 600. In the last 90 years they've been hunted to near extinction. On top of that, deforestation has robbed them of their natural habitat.

VANISHING SPECIES

Just a few of the 6,000 different animals currently threatened with extinction

SIBERIAN TIGER

Population: between 250 and 450. Food for the Siberian tiger has become increasingly scarce, meaning the tiger has to hunt over larger areas, taking it outside the nature reserve. Unfortunately, this means they often come into contact with humans — and their guns.

GIANT PANDAS

Population: 1,000. As pandas survive almost entirely on bamboo shoots and roots, their biggest threat is starvation, due to crops failing and deforestation.

HIPPOPOTAMUS

Population: 160,000. Poachers have been killing hippos for their teeth as it's hard to distinguish between hippo teeth and ivory elephant tusks.

JAVAN RHINO

Population: around 70. One of the world's most endangered species due to hunting and poaching for their horns. Also, the population of Java has increased, expanding towns into the rain forest and destroying more and more of the Javan rhino's habitat.

RABBIT BANDICOOT

Population: Unknown. This small Australian marsupial was originally known as the common rabbit bandicoot, but it's certainly not common now. Once hunted for its pelt, numbers have also dropped due to the spread of the predatory fox and a decrease in food supplies. It's now protected but still dangerously close to extinction.

BLUE WHALE

Population: fewer than 3,000. Over the last hundred years, hunting has reduced the number of blue whales by 99 percent. Now it seems unlikely the population will ever recover.

YUCK!

It's time to come clean about pollution

AIR POLLUTION

Normally you can't see air pollution, but under certain weather conditions, a dirty mist called smog hangs over cities. Exhaust fumes from cars and trucks are the cause of this poisonous pollution. Cars fitted with catalytic converters (which change harmful gases into less harmful ones) are 90 percent less polluting.

DID YOU KNOW?
Dirty water is the world's biggest killer – every year, over five million children die from dysentery, contracted from water contaminated by sewage.

ACID RAIN

Acid rain is caused by exhaust gases from power plants and road vehicles. These gases react with sunlight and air moisture to produce a rain that is acid. When it falls, acid rain causes damage wherever it lands. It raises the level of damaging substances in the soil, trees lose their leaves and die, statues have their features eaten away by the corrosive water, and lakes become so acid nothing can live in them.

◄ *Trees in Poland eaten away by acid rain*

▲ *In Sweden lime is dropped into dying lakes and on woodlands to fight acid rain.*

SEA POLLUTION

Industrial chemicals dumped in rivers move downstream to the sea and are soon absorbed by plankton. Small fish feed on the polluted plankton. They are then eaten by bigger fish, which in turn are eaten by sea-dwelling mammals, concentrating the deadly chemicals all the time.

RIVER POLLUTION

Most sewage is treated so that it is safe to pump back into the environment, but some raw sewage is still dumped into rivers and the sea. This harms plants and animal life and is suspected of causing disease among people, such as surfers, who spend a lot of time in the water.

GARBAGE

For centuries, humans have dumped garbage in the sea. Now the amount of garbage produced is enormous and includes plastics that won't decompose for hundreds of years. This plastic becomes wrapped around birds and is also mistaken for food by fish.

A GLOWING PROBLEM

Atomic energy creates waste products that remain dangerously radioactive for up to 250,000 years – that's 245,000 years longer than the sphinx has been around! Scientists used to dump big drums of atomic waste into the ocean, but this was banned in 1983. Now governments can't decide on a safe place to store this worrying waste.

DEAD LAKES

Modern farming uses huge amounts of fertilizers to increase crop yields, but a lot of it is washed into streams and lakes. This causes water plants, such as algae, to grow in large numbers. These block out the light and use up all the oxygen. Before long there isn't enough left in the water to support fish or any other water-living animals.

OIL AT SEA

Huge sea-going oil tankers have crashed in the past, causing massive oil spills. However, most oil pollution is actually caused by leaking pipelines or ships washing out their tanks. Birds caught in slicks find their feathers coated in oil and soon die. Animals that inhale the oil fumes or eat other animals caught in oil also face almost certain death.

The continuing story of the water cycle

Water can never be used up or run out completely – it keeps going around and around fueled by the sun's energy. Each stage in the water cycle is vital to the next one. That's why interference, such as pollution, threatens the whole cycle

1 Water from lakes, rivers, and oceans is evaporated by the sun and carried by air moving over the earth.

2 Water also evaporates from plants on land.

3 Water vapor rises into the atmosph until the air temperate cools down. Then it condenses into drople water, forming clouds.

4 When water vapor condenses near the ground it forms fog, mist, or dew. This moisture is often reabsorbed into the ground.

EVAPORATION

EVAPORATION

Our oceans hold about 97 percent of the world's water. A further 2 percent is frozen in the polar ice caps. This means that only about 1 percent of the world's water is going around the water cycle at any one time.

11 Rivers flow into the sea and the cycle continues.

10 Rain absorbed into the ground eventually seeps back into rivers or the sea.

6 Rain or snow on mountains may turn to ice, which will eventually melt and flow into rivers toward the sea.

5 Clouds travel on air currents. Natural [c]oling causes the water [in] the clouds to fall as [ra]in. If it's cool enough, [it] condenses into ice [cr]ystals and falls as snow.

WATER from rivers is stored in reservoirs until it is required at the water treatment works. It passes through a series of filters that remove the dirt and harmful bacteria. Then the clean water is piped through a city's water system and is ready for use.

DIRTY WATER flows into the sewer system. This sewage goes to a water treatment plant. Here, the sludge part is treated to remove bacteria and harmful gases. Then it is disposed of at sea or on the land as a fertilizer or for landfill.

The liquid part (effluent) passes through a different treatment process, again to remove the bacteria and harmful substances. The oxygen content of the effluent is increased to encourage the growth of bacteria that clean the effluent, and it is then poured into rivers to mix with the water already there.

7 Rain runs down mountains and usually ends in a river.

PERMEABLE ROCK (porous)

BRIAN WATSON

8 Rain seeps into the ground. If it falls on porous ground it seeps down until it meets nonporous rock, which stops the water sinking any further.

The level in the ground at which water collects [is ca]lled the water table.

POLLUTION SOLUTIONS

Pollution is a dirty problem, but we can all do something to clean it up

● When you go to the beach or out on a boat, make sure you take your garbage home with you. Every year a million seabirds and 100,000 marine mammals are killed because they swallow plastic or get caught in it.

● Cut down on car trips – walk or use the bus. Also, see if you can carpool with other car drivers.

● Never pour waste oil from cars down the drain or on the ground – it's a major source of pollution and poisons the water supply. Instead, find out when your town has a collection day for hazardous wastes.

● Be careful what you put down the sink and flush down the toilet.

● If you are in a car that's stuck in a long traffic jam, ask the driver to turn off the engine until the car needs to move forward. It will save gas, and you'll cut down on air pollution, too.

● Join an Adopt-A-Highway group, and help to keep a road free of litter.

● If you notice that a river is polluted by sewage, oil, or chemicals, photograph or write down what you see and report it to the Environmental Protection Agency.

● Use solar-powered products whenever possible.

● Turn off electrical appliances if they are not needed – less electricity will need to be generated and so less of the gases responsible for acid rain will be produced.

In 1987 an international conference agreed to clean up the North Sea. By 1995 the amount of harmful substances put into rivers and estuaries should be halved.

● If you like to garden, use chemicals like weed-killer and fertilizers sparingly and only according to the manufacturer's instructions. If you use extra, you are just polluting the environment.

● Keep a look out for litter around plants, and pull out any offending pieces of trash.

● Set up a local conservation group and tell people where their nearest recycling centers are.

● Find out more about nuclear energy, and ask your teachers to organize projects about the subject.

A gallon of gasoline produces 20 pounds of carbon dioxide.

● Don't leave windows open unnecessarily.

● Look out for pollution on beaches and report it to your local parks department. Alternatively, set up your own beach watch group.

POLLUTION CONTROL

NICE ONE, SUN!

The sun is like a huge power station in space. It produces so much energy that just half an hour of sunshine could provide the earth with energy for the whole year!

The most common device used to extract this energy is a solar panel. This is attached to the roof to convert the sun's light into heat. This then warms water running through pipes in the panel.

A more complicated device uses solar cells made from silicon, which convert sunlight into electricity. A university building in Newcastle, England, plans to use 450 of these solar cells to supply a third of all its electrical needs. And silicon is even used in space to power satellites. Now that's what you call a bright idea!

WATER WORKS

For centuries, water has been used to turn waterwheels to grind corn, but nowadays it's used in much more high-tech ways. Hydroelectric systems store water behind huge dams and then release it through turbines to generate electricity. The sea also has massive energy reserves waiting to be used. Within the next few years we should be able to convert the power of crashing waves into useful electricity.

WIND POWER!

Once windmills were used to grind corn or pump water out of rivers, but modern windmills just generate pollution-free electricity. At the moment, wind farms are being built all over the world in areas with regular strong breezes. However, not everyone is happy about these modern marvels. They can be quite noisy and some people feel they are just plain ugly.

Alternative energy can't solve all our problems. It's still too expensive to provide enough energy for the demands of the whole planet. But it's another step in the right direction. We've got the power – let's use it!

IT'S ONLY NATURAL!

Who needs oil, coal, or gas when you can use the pollution-free power of the sun, wind, and sea

POWER ON THE ROAD

Smog caused by cars is a common sight in Los Angeles. To combat this, it's been decided that by the year 2003, one-tenth of all new cars in California must run on electricity. Some battery-powered cars are already being tested, like this Ford Ecostar police van. It has a 100-mile range, a top speed of 70 mph and, best of all, a virtually silent engine.

INDEX